If You Were Me and Lived in...
and Lived in...
Ancient China
Han Dynasty

By Carole P. Roman

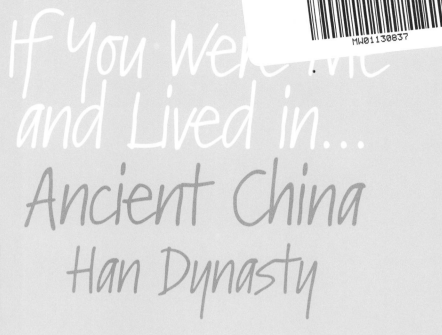

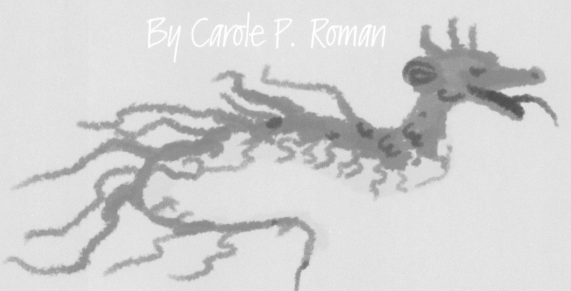

Illustrated by Mateya Arkova

For my grandmother, Laura Ross, who told a million stories and kept the past alive.

If you were me and lived in Ancient China, you would have been born almost nineteen hundred years ago in the year 150 AD.

This is what a city in China looks like now.

This is a what it might have looked like two thousand years ago.

What are some of the differences?
What has stayed the same?
How does it differ from your home?

You would have been born during the Han dynasty that ruled from 206 BC until 220 AD. A dynasty is a long line of family members that rule an area or region.

The Han dynasty was very important in Chinese history. It was one of the longest dynasties lasting over four hundred years. During its rule, the civil service was established, creating a strong and organized government. The Han Dynasty is often called the Golden Age of Ancient China. People were encouraged to write poetry and literature. Paper was invented, making it easy to read. A type of fine china called porcelain was created and exported all over the world.

If you were a boy, your parents might have chosen the name Pandi (Pan-dee) which meant *seeking a little brother,* or Yang (Ya-ng), which was the word for *ocean*. If you were a girl your name might have been Mei (May) which meant *Plum*, or Lin (Lyn) for *Jade*.

Mostly, you didn't call each other by name. Your sisters called you "Older brother," and you called them "First sister" and "Second sister."

You might have lived in the capital city Chang'an (Chang-ahn) located in central China. It was founded by the first Han emperor, Liu Bang (Loo-Bang), in 202 BC. Liu Bang was important because he was the first Chinese emperor who was a commoner. He was a politician and a strategist who led an uprising against the Qin (Chin) Dynasty.

Chang'an was a very busy city with more than 250,000 people living there. It was an economic, political, military, and cultural center for China. All important roads converged there, most importantly, a trade route called the Silk Road.

The Silk Road was a major thoroughfare that connected cities all over China to the rest of the world, making towns and their products available. Merchants traveled in caravans, bringing products to trade from foreign markets, then took Chinese exports like silk to European cities.

The Silk Road brought wealth into China, creating a new class of people called merchants. The Roman Empire sought Chinese silk, making these Chinese merchants very rich.

Your city was laid out with main streets and lots of little alleyways. The town itself was surrounded by a thick wall made of earth and rocks for protection from bandits and people who wanted to invade it. At night, gates were locked to keep the people safe. People weren't allowed to leave or enter the town after dark.

Your father was a doctor in the court of the emperor, so you lived in a very fine house with servants. You knew that the poor people lived in crowded tenements. It was dangerous to walk in the streets, and you were not allowed out without a guard for protection.

You understood you were much better off than the poor farmers who lived in the countryside. Poverty-stricken farmers could not afford to own the land they farmed, and even though they had ample food, they lived a very hard life. They had to give a portion of their crops to pay taxes to the emperor. They also had to give up one month of the year to help the government either by working on canals or city walls, do street repair, or in the military. At least they were protected if they were attacked by enemies. Craftsmen and merchants were left to fend for themselves outside the protective walls because they were considered unimportant.

Homes all over Ancient China had a lot in common. Houses were always laid out similarly. Most houses had pounded earth floors and timber frames, with walls made of wood, earth, or brick. The design of an ancient Chinese building was almost the same whether it was the home of a poor family, a wealthy family, a temple, or a palace. Differences came in size of the house, and in the quality of the interior design and decorations.

Your home was built like everyone else's in your city. Most ancient Chinese houses were arranged around a rectangular courtyard. The rich built three connected wings. The fourth side of the courtyard was usually a solid gate. This created a rectangular area protected on all four sides by the wood and earth structure of the house and gate.

Poor people could not afford big homes. Instead, they built smaller houses around an open space creating a communal courtyard always facing south. Your home was rather large, and your grandparents made their home there too.

19

Inside your home was an area partitioned off for sleeping.

There was no spot devoted to meals. You ate your meals wherever your grandmother felt like having it served on that day. When there was nice weather, your servants served the food outside in the courtyard. On rainy days, the servants pulled out lightweight screens to create walls inside your home.

The most important part of your home was the space set aside to honor the ancestors of your family who used to lived in this house. This was called a shrine. It was in the center of the house and took up an entire wall.

You brought food and presents, and both you and your grandmother placed it on the shrine. After making this offering, you all ate the delicious food and shared the presents.

The type of food people ate depended on where they made their home in China. Different regions had a vast variety of resources available.

In northern China, most people ate a grain called millet which they grounded into a flour and used for porridge. In southern China, rice was the grain of choice. Farmers kept goats, pigs, and chickens. People who lived near rivers ate a lot of seafood. Wealthy people ate more meat than the poor peasants.

Every meal was a great feast in the royal palace with no less than thirty dishes being served. The emperor ate twice a day and always alone. He enjoyed delicacies made with tender calf meat, bear paw, soups of dog meat, mountain pheasant, leopard, and a wide mix of fresh seasoned vegetables. The emperor had special hothouses that grew his vegetables in every season, and he enjoyed summer fruits in the middle of the winter. Very often they sweetened the food with honey. His wine was flavored with orchids.

Kitchens were set up in a small area or building separated from the living space or house. There was always a special place in the kitchen with a little shrine for the kitchen god, too. You were not allowed to go in there on your own. It was strictly for the servants and perhaps your grandmother.

In your house your grandmother often served chicken. The emperor insisted the local farms raise chickens, making it available to everyone. It was always on the table for honored guests and special occasions.

You knew what set your home apart from a poor one was not the dishes but the expensive spices that went into them. Chili peppers and other flavorings were included in your grandmother's recipes. Anything she made with sweet and sour sauce was your favorite.

You loved watching the family cook use chopsticks to stir the food. You liked playing with them when no one was looking, but mostly they stayed in the kitchen for preparation of the food. You had heard that some families were using them to actually eat with, and when you told your grandmother, you both had a good laugh about it!

Even though you were wealthy, you had very little furniture. What your family did have was elaborate and painted beautifully. Furniture was used in the bedroom, study, and the hall. Your furniture was made of mahogany, sandalwood, and blackwood.

Most houses had a Kang (Kah-ong) bed and yours was very grand. This was an elevated platform with an area underneath to build a fire or run piping filled with hot water or air. It was also used as your sitting and eating space.

Along the wall in your bedroom were clothing racks holding your clothing. Folding screens were used throughout the house to create privacy and separate the space.

Your father was the head of the house, and your mother and the rest of the family had to obey him all the time. Your mother took care of the children, and you knew when the time came, your parents would chose a wife for you. You had very little to say in their decision.

Your father's parents lived in the house with you, and you showed them tremendous respect all the time. They taught you many things; the most important was that you revered your ancestors. You knew that you must respect as well as pray often for them at the family shrine in the house. This was a major part of your religion called Confucianism (Kuhn-few-shan-ism), named for the teacher Confucius (Kuhn-few-shuhs).

You wore a silk tunic over pants every day. In the colder weather you wore a warm, short jacket. Your mother and sisters wore tunics too, but they were very long. They usually wore two of them. They were embroidered and richly colored in bright and happy shades. You all wore slippers on your feet instead of the straw sandals the poor people had to wear.

People liked bright colors no matter if they were rich or poor. The farmers liked to wear dark blues and grays to hide the dirt. Their clothes were made from hemp instead of the soft silk cloth you had. Certain colors were very important. Only the emperor could wear yellow. White was the color of mourning and what you wore to a funeral. Red was the color of joy and happiness, so everybody liked to wear that. Wearing silk showed the community that you were a noble as well as wealthy.

Silk was very important to China's economy. It was often used as money and traded for other things. Silk was the product of the fine fibers of a worm's cocoon. It was said that the wife of the Yellow Emperor invented silk three thousand years earlier. Her name was Leizu (Lie-zoo). A cocoon fell into her cup of tea, softened and then unraveled. She noticed it was one long thread that was both strong and soft. She discovered how to combine the silk fibers into a thread and invented a loom to turn it into a soft cloth. She planted a forest of mulberry trees for the silkworms to feed and created an empire of silk.

She invented a whole industry based on the natural substance a silkworm created when it made a cocoon.

A moth laid five hundred eggs and then died. Baby worms hatched and were fed the tasty mulberry leaves for one month until they were fat. The worms spun cocoons. The cocoons were steamed to kill the growing moth inside then rinsed in hot water to loosen the threads. Women carefully unwound the cocoons then combined six or seven fibers into silk thread. The threads were woven onto a loom and pounded to make them soft.

The process of making silk was a closely regarded secret and punishable by death if it was revealed.

China was the only place to get this new material. Once people tried the light fabric, they had to have it, no matter what the cost. People all over the world demanded the product. This made the silk merchants in China very rich.

Your mother wore her hair up with a little hat that held dangling bells that told you she was nearby. She always wore an elaborate hairstyle that took hours to prepare. Her maids coiled and braided her hair so it looked bigger than her face! Your sisters were not allowed to pin up their hair until they were married.

Your mother's face was dusted white with rice powder that made her look like a delicate doll. She had a tidy box filled with all of her make-up. Her eyebrows were darkened to stand out on her pale skin. She drew them in a high arch, so she looked surprised most of the time.

She used red rouge to paint shapes like circles or hearts over her lips. She told you that coloring lips pleased the gods, and it made everybody happy. She loved to try out new lip balms and make pretty designs over her mouth. The more she experimented, it showed neighbors she enjoyed a special status as a rich lady with time and money to try these things.

Your father shaved the sides of his head, leaving the hair in the center to grow long. He tied it in a top knot and used gold pins to keep it in place. He wore a square of cloth over it. You were growing your top knot now, but it was not as long as your father's.

Everybody had long hair. Short hair was a sign that someone had been punished. Of course, the monks in the temple shaved all hair off to show they didn't care about how they looked.

Your parents had several slaves working in the house. These people had been sold into slavery many years ago to pay off the money they owed your family. If they had children, they were slaves, as well. Life was very harsh for them. Life was very harsh for them. At least your family's slaves worked in your home and not out in the fields where it was hard la-bor. They helped your mother and grandmother with the household chores.

Sometimes slaves were prisoners captured during a war. Many worked in the fields, built roads, or in homes like yours. Some worked for noble houses or even the em-peror. They had it the worst. When the emperor or noble died, they could be killed and buried in his tomb, so they would be there to serve their master in death.

There were four major professions. Doctors, like your father, were at the top along with warriors, scholars, and advisors to the emperor. Then came farmers, artisans, and finally merchants. Fathers taught their sons, and generally, it was expected for you to be in the same profession.

Scholars were the most valued. Your father was respected. He owned a chariot and carried a sword. Farmers were next in importance because they grew the food that fed the nation. Artists and craftsmen made beautiful and useful objects and were admired for their talents. Merchants were the least respected. All they cared about was making money.

You wanted to be a noodle maker and make tasty noodles for people to enjoy. You loved watching the noodle maker create long strings of dough that stretched for miles, but your father told you you were going to be a doctor, and that was the end of that.

Your grandfather said there was an important legend of when the heavens sent some wise kings down to help man survive the harsh world. One king was a taster. He tasted all the plants to find which ones were safe and what they could do to help when someone was sick. He learned which ones could cure illnesses. He explained that this was the story of the first doctor, and it was an honor to be one. He created medicine and saved man from being sick.

Your father wanted you to read the many books and become a doctor to help people just like your father and your grandfather.

You said if you couldn't be a noodle maker, you'd like to create paper. Paper was a very important invention, you argued.

In the year 105 AD, a man by the name of Cai Lun (Cahi Lun) dipped a screen into a barrel of mashed-up pulp made from rice straw and tree shavings soaking in water. It had a layer of wet mush that was pressed and dried after the screen was raised. The end result was paper. Paper was valuable to everybody from artist to doctors and the fishmongers who needed to wrap up fish! This new invention was the most wonderful thing you had ever seen, next to noodles, that is.

School was free and available to only boys in every province. The Grand School in the capital had over thirty thousand students!

Your father hired a tutor for you at home. He invited some of the children of important nobles in the court to study with you, so you had a small group and were not lonely. He didn't want you distracted by all those children from different social classes. He felt you may pick up some bad habits.

Your sisters were taught how to be good wives and mothers. Father said it was a waste of time to educate a girl since their opinions didn't matter. You liked your first sister and didn't think that was fair, but that was life, and nothing could be done about it. You had heard that some girls were allowed to be tutored, but your father forbade it.

You argued that you had heard of a famous woman named Bao Zhao (Ban Jho) who had written a few books. She was called a female Confucius. Cai Wenji (Cahi Wen-je) wrote beautiful poems. You thought your first sister should have a chance to learn, but no one agreed.

You studied the three major religions in school. Lao-Tzu (Laow-Ta) was the founder of Taoism (To-aw-iz-em) thousands of years ago. Tao means way or path. He believed in the concept of Yin (Yin) and Yang (Ya-ng). You were taught to put your dark side and sunny side together in one circle of life. This was thought to keep a person content and in good health. Keeping your yin and yang in balance kept you happy and healthy. You achieved this by eating well, exercising, and living in a cheerful environment. Life was to be natural and spontaneous.

Confucius was born in 551 BC. He was a great philosopher and thinker. He came up with a code to live by, and many people recorded his thoughts and spread them all over China. His teachings urged treating others with respect, politeness, and fairness. He believed family was important, and you should respect and honor of your relatives. People often quoted Confucius, and you had to memorize many of his sayings. Some of your favorites were: "When anger rises, think of the consequences" or "Forget injuries, never forget kindness." You quoted him when your tutor criticized the speed of your work. You told him, "It does not matter how slowly you go as long as you don't stop."

Buddhism (Bu-diz-em) was the third religion you studied. It was created by a prince in Nepal (Ne-pal), just south of China in the 6th Century BC. Buddhism was about the rebirth of the self. They taught that a person must come back again and again until they learned how to live a proper life; only then could their soul enter nirvana. Buddha (Boo-da) believed in karma (kar-ma), that any actions you take can come back to either help or harm you. If a person behaved badly, they might have something bad happen to them. If they were kind, then karma would be kind to them.

You also studied poetry and how to write using a special brush. This was called calligraphy (cal-lig-ruh-fee).

You learned to use the grand brushstrokes for the many Chinese characters. Each character could represent both sound and meaning. There were multiple characters for each symbol, each one having a different meaning. Each character could represent one syllable of spoken Chinese, part of a word, or even be a word on its own. There were thousands of characters to memorize. You had to be both smart and artistic.

When you weren't in school, you played with many toys. When you were younger, you had colorful marbles and small carved figures of dragons and other animals. Your sisters had dolls and masks. You both played with puppets. You loved any toy that made noise, and many were filled with seeds, so they rattled.

You also had a collection of whistles and flutes made from bamboo. You had a sword too. You enjoyed playing the board game known as "Go" or Zh-wéiqí (Wey-chee) with your schoolmates. You learned it by watching all the men move the stones around the black and white checkerboard. It is a game of strategy, and all gentlemen knew how to play.

Your favorite possession was the colorful dragon kite you flew in the wind with your father. Your grandfather made it from silk and bamboo, and it was the most impress-ive one in the sky.

Music was very important to bring harmony into people's lives. You loved hearing the bells and chimes. They used flutes and a stringed instrument called a gungin (gewgin), which made you thoughtful when you heard it.

Your father took you to see dancers as well. They combined acrobatics and dance movements with juggling, martial arts, and music to do lots of fascinating stunts. You loved going to see these shows.

The Lantern Festival was the last day of your most important holiday, called the Spring Festival or Chinese New Year. It took place on the first full moon in the Chinese calendar, marking the return of spring.

The holiday began when an emperor saw Buddhist monks lighting lanterns to show respect for Buddha on the fifteenth day of the first lunar month. He ordered that every household and temple should do the same thing. It became a holiday where people got together to light the colorful lanterns and celebrate with fun activities like stilt walking, fireworks, and lion dances.

Children held small lights while walking in the street enjoying the huge, elaborate decorations made up to look like animals, fruit, birds, or flowers. Symbolically lighting the colorful beacons was like illuminating the future. People prayed for good fortune to come their way when they participated.

The lion was seen as a strong and brave animal. The lion dance was performed to drive away evil. You watched two men underneath the huge costume dance to the beat of a drum, gong, and cymbals. Sometimes they were very funny, but you remembered being afraid of the great lion when you were younger.

Numbers were important to you. The numbers two, three, five, eight, and nine were considered lucky. The number two because good things came in pairs. The word for three sounded like the word birth, and that was a special event. Five represented the five elements of Chinese philosophy: fire, water, earth, metal, and wood. Eight was the luckiest number because it sounded like the word prosper, which meant to do well. Lastly, nine sounded a lot like long life and was always associated with dragons and the emperor. Six and seven were lucky numbers too.

The number four was unlucky because it sounded like the word death. Fourteen sounded like "want to die" in Chinese, so it was always unlucky.

You picked colors based on their importance as well. Red was the color of fire and represented the summer. It symbolized good luck, success, and happiness. Your mother wore a red dress to her wedding.

Black was the color of water and the winter. It was used for the color of heaven and the favorite color of the Emperor Qin.

Green represented the color of spring, so it brought happiness.

White was the color of metal and the fall. It was not considered lucky, and the color was worn when someone died to honor them.

Yellow was the color of the earth and was used to show the change of seasons. Only the emperor wore yellow.

60

61

You were born during the Year of the Horse. The Chinese calendar was represented by one of twelve animals tied to the year you were born and had a special meaning to you as a person.

You were told that you possess many of the traits of the animal for your birth. The twelve animals are the rat, ox, tiger, rabbit, dragon, snake, horse, goat, monkey, rooster, dog, and pig.

You were proud to tell everyone that you were hardworking, popular, and cheerful but can be stubborn and not listen to advice. Still you would rather be born in the Year of the Horse than the year of of the Rat like your sister, who could be charming but sneaky!

So you see , if you were me how life in the Han dynasty in Ancient China could really be.

Important People
in the Ancient China

Ban Zhao (Ban Jho)- (45-c118 AD)- first known female Chinese historian. She completed her brother's book on the history of Western Han, the *Book of Han*. She also wrote *Lessons for Women*, a book advising women how to honor their relationship as a wife. She wrote poems and essays and was interested in astronomy and mathematics. She was China's most famous scholar.

Cai Lun (Cahi Lun)- (50- 121 AD)- a Han dynasty official regarded as the person who invented paper and the paper-making process. He said he was inspired by the way paper wasps made their nests.

Cai Wenji (Cahi Wen-je)- (117- 250 AD)- female poet born two thousand years ago.

Emperor Han Mindgi (Em-per-er Han Ming-ti)- (28- 75 AD)- the second emperor of the Eastern Chinese Han dynasty.

Genghis Khan (Geng-ges Kang)- (1162- 1227 AD)- was the founder and great emperor of the Mongol Empire, which became the largest empire in history.

Hua Mulan (Hwah Moo-lawn)- (420- 589 AD)- a legendary female warrior first described in a ballad known as the Ballad of Mulan. In this song, Hua Mulan takes her father's place in the army. She was known for her skills at Kung Fu and sword fighting.

Leizu (Lie-zoo)- (C 3000 BC)- a legendary Chinese empress and wife of the Yellow Emperor. According to tradition, she discovered silk and invented the silk loom in the 27th century BC.

Sun Tzu (Sun Tsue)- (544-496 BC)- Chinese general, strategist, and philosopher who lived in Ancient China. He is credited with writing the famous book, *The Art of War*.

Qin Shi Huang (Chin Shi Hwang)- (260-210 BC)- became the first emperor of Qin after conquering all the warring factions. He united all of China in 221 BC.

Wu Zetian (Woo Ze-chan)- (624- 705 AD)- the only female empress to rule in four thousand years of Chinese history.

Glossary

alleyway (al-ley-way)- a passage between buildings.

ancestor (an-ces-tor)- one of the people from whom a person is descended.

artisan (ar-ti-san)- a person who is skilled at making things by hand.

bamboo (bam-boo)- a tall plant with hard hollow stems that are used for buildings or making furniture.

blackwood (black-wood)- any of several hardwood trees.

Buddha (Boo-da)- the title given to Siddartha Gautama, the founder of Buddhism. He was born as a prince but decided to give up his crown, riches, and family to become a monk. He learned how to meditate and taught others of his new found religion and beliefs.

Buddhism (Bu-diz-em)- a religion of eastern and central Asia that is based on the teachings of Gautama Buddha.

calf (kaf)- young cow.

calligraphy (cal-lig-ra-fee)- the art of making beautiful letters when handwriting.

caravan (ker-uh-van)- a group of pack animals used as transportation to sell and trade goods from town to town.

Chang'an (Chang-ahn)- an ancient capital of more than ten dynasties in Chinese history, today known as Xi'an. Chang'an means "Perpetual Peace" in Classical Chinese.

chariot (char-i-ot)- a carriage with two wheels that was pulled by horses and was raced and used in battle in ancient times.

chopsticks (chop-stik)- two thin sticks used largely in Asia to bring food to the mouth to eat

cocoon (co-coon)- a housing typically created out of silk that a few insects (like caterpillars) form around themselves to protect them while they grow.

communal (com-mun-al)- shared in common by a group.

Confucius (Kuhn-few-shuhs)- (551-479 BC)- China's most famous teacher, philosopher, and political theorist, whose ideas have influenced the civilization of East Asia.

Confucianism (Kuhn-few-shan-ism)- of or relating to the Chinese philosopher Confucius or his teachings or followers.

court (ko-rt)- the residence or establishment of a king or ruler.

courtyard (ko-rt-yard)- an enclosure adjacent to a building such as a house or palace.

dynasty (di-ne-stee)- a family of rulers who rule over a country for a long period of time.

embroider (em-broi-der)- to sew a design on a piece of cloth.

emperor (em-per-er)- a man who rules an empire.

fibers (fi-bers)- a thin thread of natural or artificial material that can be used to make cloth and paper.

"Go "encircling game" (Go "en-circle-ing game")- an abstract strategy board game for two players, where the goal is to take over more area than the opponent also known as- Zh-wéiqíi (Wey-chee).

gugin (gew-gin)- a seven-string Chinese musical instrument of the zither family that the player plucks rather than strums.

Han (Han)- spanning over four centuries, the Han period is considered a golden age in Chinese history.

hemp (hemp)- a plant that is used to make thick ropes.

hereditary (he-red-uh-ta-ree)- holding a position or title that was passed on from your parent or an older relative.

hothouse (hot-haus)- a greenhouse maintained at a high temperature, especially for the culture of tropical plants.

Kang (Kah-ong)- a bed-like structure made from a long, raised platform of bricks and clay materials. It is used for working, living, sleeping and entertaining.

karma (kar-ma)- the concept of by doing good, good things will come back to you, verses by doing bad, bad things will come back to you.

Lao-Tzu (Laow-Ta)- an ancient Chinese philosopher and writer who created Taoism.

legend (le-jend)- a story from the past that is believed by many people but cannot be proven true.

Lin (Lyn)- a popular girl's name in Ancient China that means jade.

Liu Bang (Loo-Bang)- (c 247-195 BC)- first emperor of the Han dynasty.

lip balm (lip baum)- colored paste cosmetic for the lips.

loom (lum)- machinery or a frame that allows yarn or threading to create cloth.

lunar (lun-er)- measured by the moon's revolution around the earth.

mahogany (me-ha-gan-ee)- a tropical reddish-brown wood used for furniture.

Mei (May)- popular girl's name in Ancient China that means plum.

millet (mil-let)- type of grass that is grown for its seeds which are used as food.

Mongol (Mon-gol)- a member of any of a group of traditionally pastoral peoples of Mongolia.

monk (menk)- a man who is a member of a religious order and lived in a monastery. His whole life is devoted to religion.

monastery (mon-as-te-ree)- a place where monks live and work together.

mourning (mor-ning)- great sadness felt because someone has died.

mulberry tree (mul-ber-ree tree)- the leaves from this tree are a favorite meal for silkworms.

Nepal (Ne-pal)- a country located in South Asia where Buddha was born.

nirvana (ner-va-na)- the state of perfect happiness and peace in Buddhism where there is release from all forms of suffering.

noodle maker (nud-el-mak-er)- a high skilled worker who makes very long noodles for eating.

offering (of-fer-ing)- something that is given to God or a god as a part of religious worship.

orchid (or-ked)- a plant with flowers that are brightly colored and have unusual shapes.

Pandy (Pan-dee)- a popular boy's name in Ancient China that means wants *little brother*.

philosopher (fi-las-so-fer)- a person who studies culture and why people do the things they do.

porcelain (por-ce-lain)- hard, fine-grained, sonorous, nonporous, and usually translucent and white ceramic ware.

porridge (pawr-idge)- a soft food made by boiling meal of grains or legumes in milk or water until thick.

pulp (puhlp)- a soft, wet substance that is made by crushing something.

Qin Dynasty (Chin Dy-nas-ty)- from 246 BC through 206 BC, the Qin Dynasty was the first to unify the imperial government and build a lot of the Great Wall in China.

revere (rev-eare)- to have great respect for someone or something.

sandalwood (san-del-wood)- wood with a sweet smell that is regularly used to manufacture carved items as well as produce oils used in the forming of soaps and perfumes.

scholars (skal-ers)- a student who has studied a particular subject and has deep knowledge on said subject.

shrine (sh-rine)- a place that people visit because it is connected with someone or something that is important to them.

silk (sil-k)- smooth, soft, and shiny cloth that is made from thread produced by silkworms.

Silk Road- an ancient trade route that extended from China to the Mediterranean Sea.

strategy (strad-e-gee)- a careful plan or method for achieving a particular goal usually over a long period of time.

syllable (sil-uh-bul)- any one of the parts into which a word is naturally divided when it is pronounced.

Tao (Ta-ow)- is a Chinese philosophy in which universal ideals shape the way of life and human action.

Taoism (Ta-ow-iz-em)- a religious or philosophical tradition of Chinese origin that emphasizes living in harmony with the Tao (also known as Dao). The term Tao means way, path, or principle.

temple (tem-pel)- a building for religious practice.

tenement (ten-uh-ment)- a large building that has apartments or rooms for rent and is usually in a poorer part of a city.

tomb (toom)- a building or chamber above or below the ground in which a dead body is kept.

top knot (top-not)- the tuft of hair on the top of the head.

tunic (too-nick)- a loose piece of clothing usually without sleeves that reaches to the knees and worn by men and women.

Yang (Ya-ng)- a popular boy's name in Ancient China and is also the word for ocean.

yang (ya-ng)- the idea that contrary forces compliment each other. They are understood as two halves that complete each other. Yang is sunny to yin's shady side.

yin (yin)- the idea that contrary forces compliment each other. They are understood as two halves that complete each other. Yin is the shady side to yang's sunny side.

Printed in the USA
CPSIA information can be obtained
at www.ICGtesting.com
LVHW070824101023
760648LV00001B/1